The Complete Harmonica Player

Wise Publications
London/New York/Paris/Sydney/Copenhagen/Madrid

Exclusive Distributors:
Music Sales Limited
8/9 Frith Street,
London W1V 5TZ, England.
Music Sales Pty Limited
120 Rothschild Avenue,
Rosebery, NSW 2018,
Australia.

Order No.AM89718
ISBN 0-7119-3058-9
This book © Copyright 1993 by Wise Publications

Cover design by Studio Twenty, London
Cover photography by George Taylor
Computer management by Adam Hay Editorial Design
Compiled by John Tyler
Printed in the United Kingdom by
J.B. Offset Printers (Marks Tey) Limited, Marks Tey, Essex.
Photographs courtesy of Matth. Hohner AG

Part 1

Introduction

Learning to play the harmonica (or mouth organ) is a lot of fun. This tutor is rather special in the way it teaches you to play. Part 2, especially, contains many popular standards.

We intend you to be successful! Many people who have taken up the harmonica have not been able to progress very far. One big difficulty is getting good single notes.

If you are holding the Hohner **Meisterklasse** harmonica you have a built-in bonus in learning to play, although this tutor may be used with any C harmonica (including chromatics) if hole one blowing is middle C. These would be the **Cross Harp, Pro Harp, Blues Harp** and the **CX12**.

We'll deal with chromatic harmonicas in Part 2. In addition there are various kinds of **diatonic harmonicas** which are different in layout from the Hohner range.

You will recognise a chromatic harmonica by the slide at the end of it. As the notes of the Meisterklasse are laid out in exactly the same way as the chromatic, it will be easy to progress to the advanced instrument at a later stage. You will have heard the harmonica on radio, record, TV and films. Now, it's your turn to play.

Meisterklasse

Cross Harp

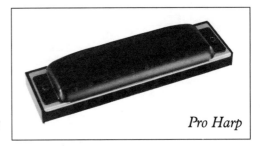

Pro Harp

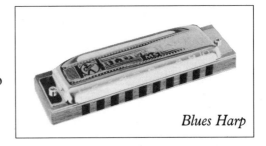

Blues Harp

CX12

First Steps to Playing

Warming Up

Take your harmonica in your hand with the hole numbers on the top plate facing you. To do the job properly, warm the harmonica before you play it: hold the mouthpiece in the palm of your hand.

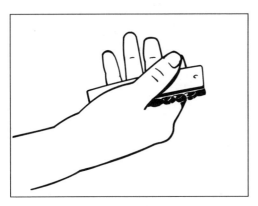

After a few minutes, it is ready for playing. The harmonica is new, so blow and draw gently. Put the harmonica to your mouth and blow a mouthful of notes – gently! If that sounded too heavy or too breathy, try to take it nice and easy, and relax. Breathiness can be cured by keeping an air-tight seal round the notes.

Take another look at your harmonica. Hold it in a comfortable way and let your lips find the hole marked **5**. Now blow into it gently but firmly. Then, keeping very relaxed – don't gasp at it! – draw in hole **5**. Now blow and draw gently a few times in hole **5**. Keep that air-tight but relaxed mouth formation round the hole.

Stop for now. The next job is very important: tap the moisture from the mouth organ on to the palm of the hand.

To start with, have the harmonica out for a few minutes at a time and repeat this sequence.

Now for something new. Blow and draw in hole **5**; then do exactly the same in hole **6**. You have now found four notes and, as they are repeated lower down, that means eight notes out of the sixteen on your harmonica!

Put the notes you have learnt together – like this: hole **5** blow/draw, hole **6** blow/draw. Did that sound a little familiar? It is the first half of a scale and it looks like this:

There is a lot in that little picture and you'll pick up the special language of music as you go along. Just for now, enjoy getting four clear notes. Then you can play this to a count of four.

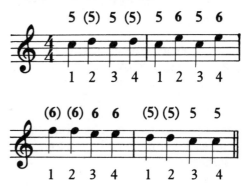

Notice you moved from **6** blow to **5** blow. Make this smooth by moving the harmonica and *not* your head.

How about trying this fun tune entitled 'Student's Stomp'? The curves over the music are known as **phrase marks** and they act like punctuation in language. Try it:

Make each note sharp and clear, then you will know that you are sounding single notes – but not too loudly!

Just look at that tune for a moment. It is written on or between lines which are known as the **stave.**

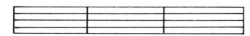

The sign at the beginning $\left[\begin{smallmatrix}\clubsuit\end{smallmatrix}\right]$ is a **G** or **treble clef**.

The four **crotchets** (or quarter notes) to a bar are shown by the time signature, (**C**), also called **common time** and often written as $\frac{4}{4}$.

Each **bar** is marked by a **bar line**. In $\frac{4}{4}$ time, each bar must add up to four crotchet beats.

Think about all that now, as you play this next tune called 'Happy Days'.

Now for two forward steps.

First, look at the harmonica and hole 7. Draw and blow in that hole a few times. Then it's up the scale for two more steps. Like this:

Now you know six notes out of eight. That's twelve out of sixteen! Are the single notes coming easily?

You have seen that each crotchet is worth one beat. Another note, a **minim**, $\left(\,\rule{0pt}{1.5ex}\right)$ is worth two crotchet beats but is only sounded once.

Here it is in a tune called 'Lazy Days'.

In the first tune below, 'Hobbies', we use crotchets and minims again but this time we count *two* crotchet beats to the bar.

In the second tune we count *three* crotchet beats to the bar, as shown.

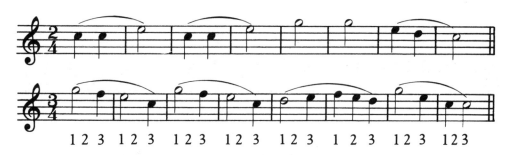

1 2 3 1 2 3 1 2 3 1 2 3 1 2 3 1 2 3 1 2 3 1 2 3

Notes, Rests and Ties

Go back over all the work you have done so far and be sure of all the steps. You come now to a different order of notes. So far it has been blow/draw, blow/draw, blow/draw, but at hole **8**, there is a change. It is *draw/blow*. Try it a few times to get used to it then, very smoothly, moving only the harmonica, play:

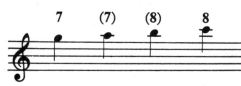

Now has come the time to give each note its proper name:

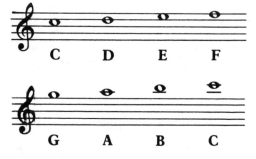

Ready to move on to some new tunes?

These introduce **quavers**, (), which are half the value of a crotchet, so two quavers equal one crotchet.

♪ ♪ = ♩

They may be joined like this:

Here are the **rests** to go with the notes:

━ minim

𝄽 crotchet

𝄾 quaver

Watch out for them!

When two adjacent notes of the *same* pitch are joined by a **tie** (see ＊ in 'Wooden Heart'), only the first note is sounded and that sound prolonged into the second. A tie acts like an addition sign. Thus, ⌢♩ is worth five beats.

Wooden Heart

Second Steps to Playing

Single Note Playing

The Meisterklasse has made it easy for you to get single notes. Now I want you to try to use your tongue. You may use a 'whistle' method but the tongue is better. Try hole 5. Block off the holes to the left with your tongue. Use your lip to block the other side, like this:

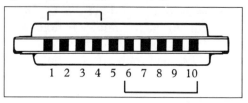

Holding the Harmonica

Now, to hold the harmonica properly. Place it in your left hand like this:

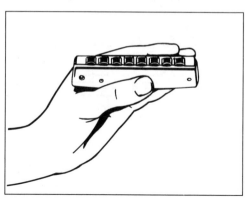

Bring your right hand round like this:

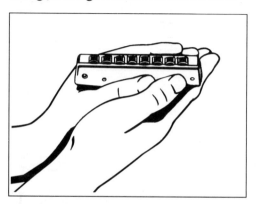

Always use this playing position from now on.

You will have noticed that we have used the numbers on the top cover plate to guide us. However, playing by numbers is *not* playing by music, so don't rely on them too much. Music is a language and it is not too difficult to learn it – if you approach it in the right way. A music teacher will always be pleased to help with the theory.

Some Musical Terms

Here are some expression marks for you to learn. It won't take long to get used to them but it is very important for you to know them in order to 'read' music

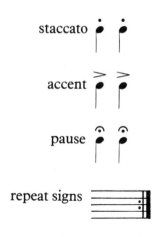

diminuendo ▷ (get softer)
crescendo ◁ (get louder)

There are many, many Italian words that you will meet and I recommend that you study the rudiments of music. Here are a few common ones:

piano (p) – soft
forte (f) – loud
andante – an easy walking pace
allegro – quick, lively

The Scale of C Major

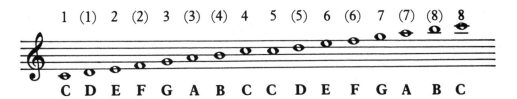

The above music shows the whole range of your harmonica in notation.

Now you've worked at the upper scales, look at the lower ones. Before you play these tunes, notice we have two **C**'s in the middle of the harmonica in holes **4** and **5**. Choose one. Don't play them both or they will sound unpleasant.

Amazing Grace

 is a **triplet** and means three notes played in the time normally taken to play two.

We'll return to this tune later on.

Down In The Valley

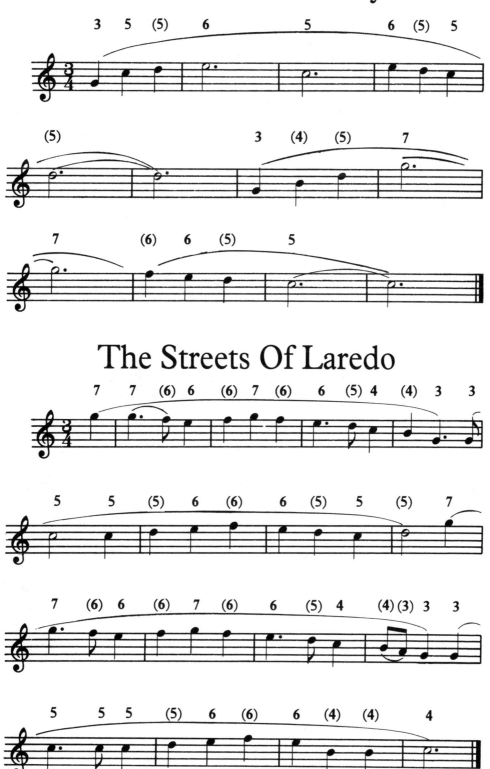

The Streets Of Laredo

Morning Has Broken

We'll go now to the lowest notes. Play the first tunes again using these notes: they are eight notes or an **octave** lower than before. Don't blow too hard – keep it gentle but firm. Check for clarity of sound.

Try these well-known tunes in the lower register.
Watch out for all you have learnt about note values and so on.

Puff (The Magic Dragon)

Before we play 'Puff', there are two points to consider. First, dotted notes. A dot after a note makes that note half as long again. Thus, in bar 4, the dotted minim (𝅗𝅥.) equals 𝅗𝅥 + 𝅘𝅥

Second, in bars 5 and 13, the natural accent is displaced by the quaver/ dotted crotchet rhythm. These are tricky bars and will need a bit of extra work. Don't forget to count. Notice also the repeat sign at the end of the piece. This time, chord symbols are given – so ask a guitarist or banjo picker to play along with you!

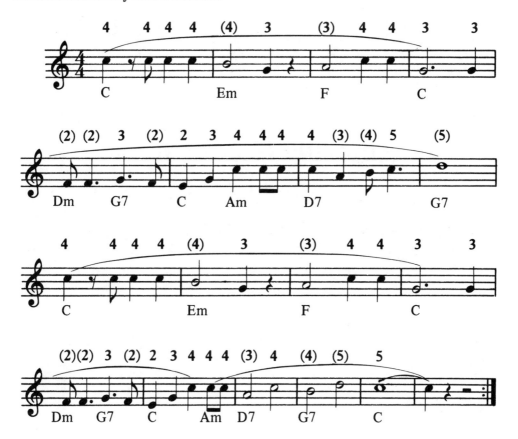

Key Signatures

All the tunes so far have been in the key of C major. The relative minor of C major is **A minor,** and the following melody in that key will help you with the lower notes.

It is possible to play in Keys other than C on the Student Harmonica. There are twelve major keys altogether, and each one has its own key signature. For example, the key of **F major** has one flat and **G major** has one sharp.

F major   G major

Amazing Grace (in F)

Amazing Grace (in G)

The Yellow Rose Of Texas

The Vibrato

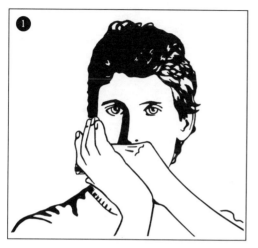

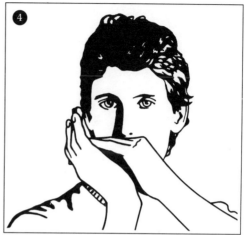

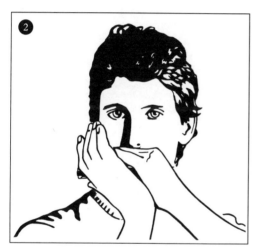

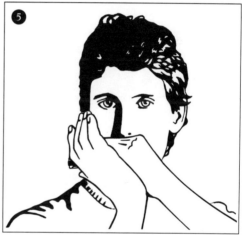

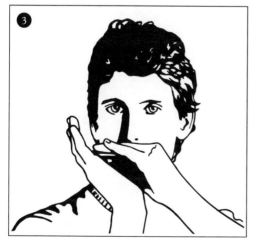

Another musical device is the **vibrato**. This is achieved by gently opening and closing the hands – slowly. A fast 'wah-wah' sound is very ugly to listen to. Either the right or left hand may be used. I always use the left so that the right is free for the slide on the chromatic harmonica.

Part 2

Part 2

If you have studied Part I thoroughly, you will already know many tunes and I hope will be able to play anything in C using the notes on the Student Harmonica.

Moving to the chromatic harmonica is a big and exciting step. Check that you can still remember all the things you have learned so far.

Are you looking after the instrument? Can you hear good, clear, single notes? Are you using your hands properly? Are you now able to play with a full tone and open throat?

Keep the harmonica well back in the mouth. Remember, the sound matters most of all. Brilliant note playing can be ruined by poor tone.

You have now chosen the way of obtaining single notes that suits you best. Remember, the tongue blocking method offers the chance of playing octaves and other intervals and, in my view, gives a richer sound, allowing more control of the instrument.

The CX12

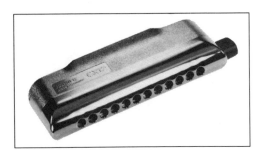

This instrument has long been popular in this country with professionals and good amateurs. The first eight holes of the Meisterklasse harmonica are the same as the CX12, but without the slide.

Holes 9-12 of the CX12 offer the next octave up, like this:

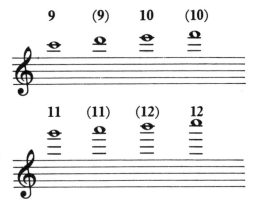

The 16 hole model has many fans amongst professionals in the USA and on the Continent.

The CX12 is recommended for its easy slide action and good tone.

Warming Up

Remember to take your harmonica in your left hand with the hole numbers on the top plate facing you. To do the job properly, warm the harmonica before you play it by holding the mouthpiece in the palm of your hand.

Now you've bought your chromatic, go back over all the music played in Part I. Now try these two new melodies. Make sure the chromatic is well warmed as it takes a bit more effort to get a good sound.

You should be able to work at the tunes *without* using the numbers except from time to time as a prop.

From Both Sides Now

King Of The Road

Watch the rests!

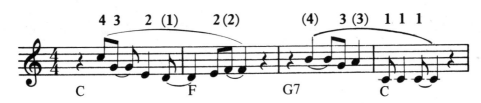

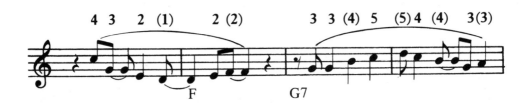

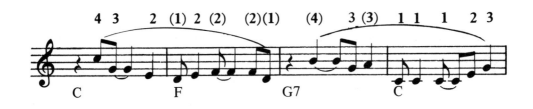

Other Major Keys

You will remember that there are 12 major scales, all sharing the same basic structure:

TONE TONE SEMITONE TONE

TONE TONE SEMITONE

By way of example, look again at the scale of C major:

In order to retain this structure, subsequent major scales are modified by the addition of sharps or flats.

Start with **F major:** the fourth note is **Bb** and you get it by playing hole **3** draw with the slide in. Have your index finger on the slide already and keep your hands in the correct playing position.

Now play the scale of **F major** up and down. (→) means put the slide in.

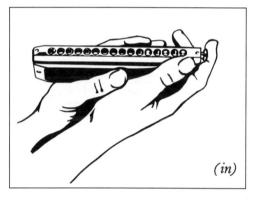

(in)

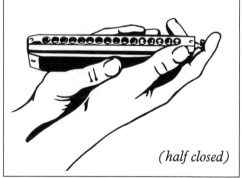

(half closed)

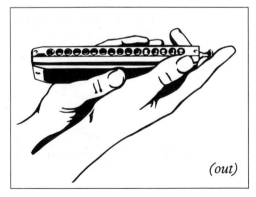

(out)

25

I'd Like To Teach The World To Sing

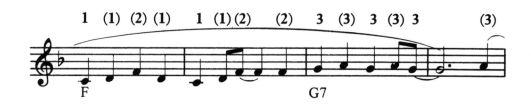

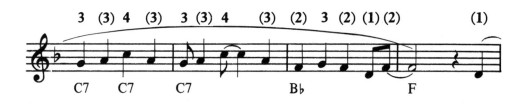

Playing Tips

Now for a few tips. On a chromatic harmonica two little tricks will help you to save breath. (In fact you can edit your own music.)

Every **F** in a draw hole can also be obtained by blowing in the same hole with the slide in (except hole 10 on the **Educator II** when the blow note is **G**).

Every **C**, except **middle C** on the Chrometta 8 and the Super Chromonica, may be obtained by drawing in the same hole with the slide in.

This does not apply to the very top hole: the draw note is **D** = an extra note.

Accidentals

Another musical device is to put a sharp sign (♯) to raise or a flat sign (♭) to lower the note that follows immediately after the sign. The natural sign (♮) restores a note that was previously sharp or flat to a natural one. These are called **accidentals** and they generally occur when notes are required that fall outside the home key.

Here to help you is a beautiful melody that will enhance every facet of your playing. It will need a great deal of work. Play it with a good tone and use the vibrato tastefully.

Watch the natural **B** and sharpened **C**. You will find **C♯** in holes **4** or **5** blowing with the slide in. Hole **5** is the better choice here. Chord symbols for guitar, banjo, and the like are included. Try playing it with somebody else: **you'll** enjoy the experience.

The accidentals are marked with a slide mark (→). The hole numbers with a bracket are draw notes.

Yesterday

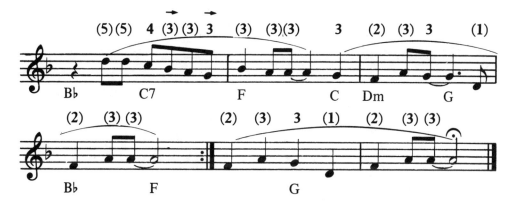

Tie A Yellow Ribbon
'Round The Ole Oak Tree

Let the slide in and out clearly and precisely.

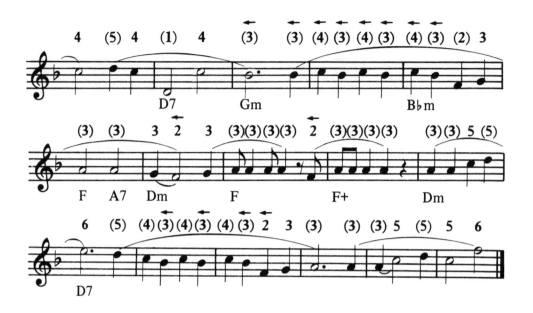

Spanish Flea (in C)

Key of G Major

It's now time to look at the key of
G major. Here is the scale. Notice the
F♯ is a draw note with the slide in.

Streets Of London

Breathe in a relaxed manner

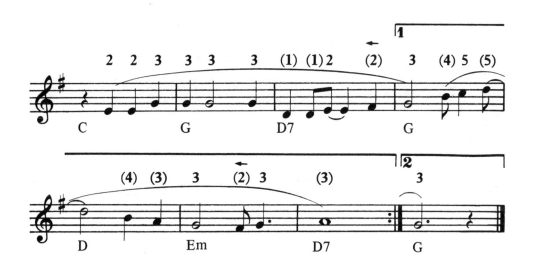

Leaving On A Jet Plane

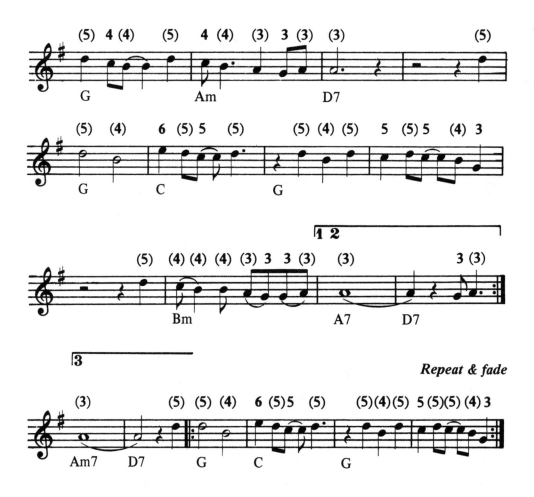

Gonna Build A Mountain

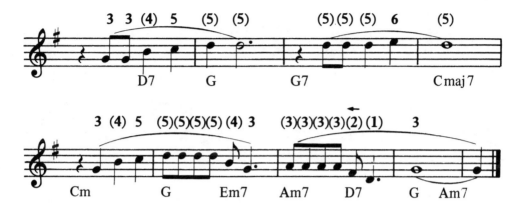

Try this one again but an octave higher this time. Start with hole **5** draw. Let it swing.

D and Eb Majors

We are now going to learn two more keys and their scales – **D** and **E♭ majors**.

D major

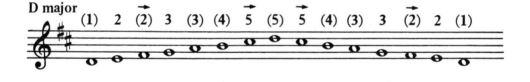

E♭ major

A slow ballad in **Eb** will test your tone and phrasing. It suits the plaintive nature of the harmonica superbly. Get all the emotion you can from this melody. Watch the repeat signs and keep the dotted notes smooth. Notice when to use the slide. If you have the Super Chromonica, there is a low **Bb** that is a problem. You will have to come down to the **C** from hole **3** drawing with the slide in.

Can't Help Falling In Love

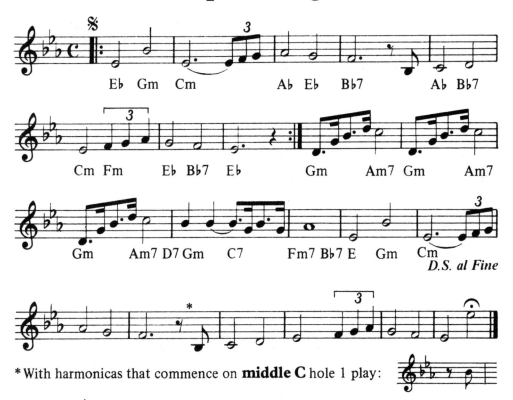

*With harmonicas that commence on **middle C** hole 1 play:

The low **B♭** is below **middle C,**
drawing with the slide in. It is not
numbered as it varies on different
models.

Bb Major

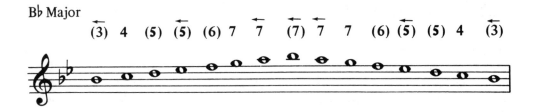

Theme From A Summer Place

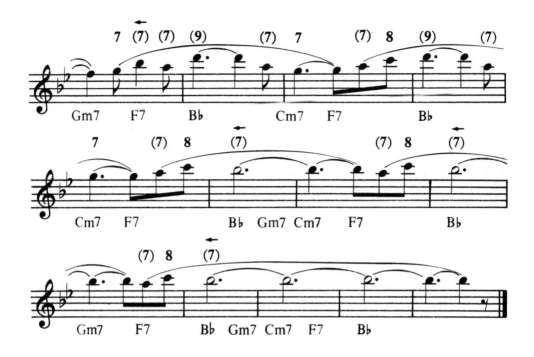

Scales for Reference

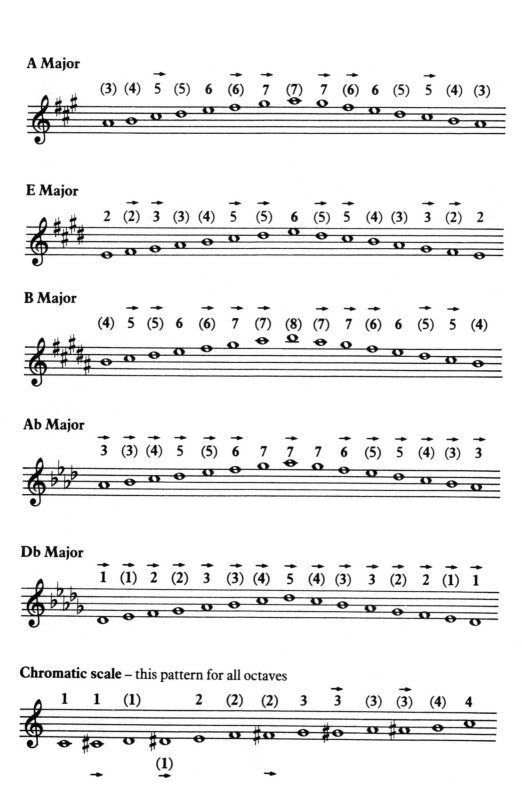

Yellow Submarine

The Midnight Special

Scarborough Fair

Where Have All The Flowers Gone

When I'm Sixty Four

Swing Low, Sweet Chariot

Blowin' In The Wind

Summary

You are now a very well established player. If you have been using your hands properly you may have discovered that with the hands open you get a good firm sound that can be muted by playing with the hands together.

(open)

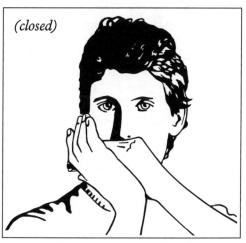

(closed)

Harmonica Music

You can now play from any music book, following either the special melody line or the top line of the piano part. You can have endless hours of fun sharing music with your friends and you can join any combination of instruments – provided you are all in tune with each other!

There is a wealth of music in the classics as well as standards and pop. Start with the easier graded music for violin, flute or oboe. As you progress, you will find much suitable music that is published for these instruments.

Keep at it. Listen to yourself *very critically.* Practise your scales. Take great care with your tone. Here's to a lifetime of music making.

Care and Maintenance

With care, a harmonica will last years. If you are doing a great deal of playing I suggest that you get two or three instruments – if money allows – and alternate them. They are still very cheap by musical instrument standards!

Remember, the more gently you blow a new harmonica, the longer it will last.

Some Harmonica History

It is worth remembering that the harmonica developed from an instrument some 5,000 years ago. By that standard, most other musical instruments are very modern!

The invention of a free reed instrument called the sheng (lit. 'sublime voice') is usually attributed to the Chinese explorer Nya-Kwa about 3,000 BC. Shengs come in various sizes and the Chinese and Japanese culture that produced them is still very much alive: sheng ensembles have given recitals in Britain during recent years.

In the early 19th Century, Christian Friedrich Ludwig Buschmann assembled the first mouth organ (probably the most accurate description of the instrument). Buschmann's invention, known as the *Mund Aeoline*, was picked up by Christian Messner, who was so fascinated by it that he produced copies on a commercial basis.

However, Messner was not into the big time; that was left to Matthias Hohner, a clockmaker whose mouth organ-making cottage industry rapidly developed into a factory one, producing millions of harmonicas to be sold all around the world.

The basic instrument was so constructed that the player could accompany himself in a simple way. However, the challenge to build a more versatile instrument could not be ignored and the chromatic harmonica came into being.

This instrument, which continues to be developed and perfected, is basically two harmonicas put together in one body.

One reed plate is tuned to C major, the other to Cb major. Judicious use of the slide enables the player to perform in any key.

The different models have given rise to a wide variety of playing styles. Larry Adler, the man who gave the harmonica concert hall status, plays a chromatic instrument. Belgian born Jean 'Toots' Thielmans became another chromatic virtuoso, this time in the jazz style.

The small ten-hole vamper - 'the harp' - is the celebrated blues instrument. Here the players divide into two camps: there is the country blues style as exemplified by Sonny Terry, and the amplified Chicago-style blues of players like Little Walter.

Harmonica groups, such as The Monarchs, The Dutch Hotcha Trio and The Jerry Murad Harmonicats, also developed a characteristic style which they owed to their use of chromatic, chord and bass instruments in ensemble.

The sound of the harmonica pervades a great deal of music. Listen out for its unique timbre, and try to hear some of the work of the instrument's great stylists - it will help improve your technique.

And, hopefully, with the aid of *The Complete Harmonica Player* a whole new world of music will open up to you.

3/94 (17406)